Light For Africa
Musafare T Mupanduki, Ph.D.

CHAPTERS

CHAPTER ONE: THE AFRICAN DILEMA

CHAPTER TWO: PROBLEM OF THE INHERITED STATE

CHAPTER THREE: THE PRE-COLONIAL LEGACY

CHAPTER FOUR: THE POST-COLONIAL LEGACY

CHAPTER FIVE: GREATER AFRICAN EFFECTIVE
PARTICIPATION IN THE   INTERNATIONAL FORUM

CHAPTER SIX: THE REVOLUTIONARY DIMENSION

CHAPTER SEVEN: THE WAY I SEE IT

Prelude

It is with a view to throwing light on the issues of African developmental that this analysis, wish to differ from other analyses on the African problem. My analysis gives an exclusive priority to the articulation of an African as opposed to a Western or foreign perspective on trends and events in Africa emphasizing the often-neglected historical dimension. The objectives of this analysis is therefore to:

♠ Critically and self-critically analyze past development experience in Africa.

♠ Examine the role of internal forces in the present crisis in Africa.

♠ Encourage the emergency of a new alternative Africa perspective on future developments in the continent.

♠ Identify ways and means of more effectively tapping Africa's largely underutilized or poorly utilized potential, both human and material.

♠ Redefine the role of the state in African development and its relations to groups and institutions in society.

CHAPTER ONE
THE AFRICAN DILEMA

After decades of domination, the dominated in Africa have developed massive inferiority feelings. These feelings manifest themselves in an acute dependency on their colonial masters, a state, which can only be redeemed by a decisive act of a program of massive continuation education awareness campaign reaching all progressive forces in the African continent.

One of the greatest paradoxes of all time is that, the richest and the most generously endowed continent in the universe has the poorest people. There are great opportunities everywhere, but Africa is too blind to see that its people literally walk on gold and yet they are too ignorant to stoop and collect the treasure. Africans sit and wait for the colonial master (under the guise of foreign direct investment) to come to their aid, forgetting that the immutable law of the universe is survival of the fittest.

In spite of the vast stretches of the Sahara and Kalahari deserts, Africa has more arable and pastureland than the U.S.A., the Soviet Union or China and India, all put together. African lands are fertile and require, at the initial stage of use, little fertilization. Such great rivers as the

Nile, the Congo, the Zambezi, and the Volta richly water these lands.

Africa has 53 of the world's most important and basic minerals and metals but Africans do not know what to do with them besides shipping and airlifting these treasures of Africa to foreign lands in exchange for a pittance. Africans again import these same materials in one form or the other at a hundred times the original value. To sell tobacco is pardonable, but to sell minerals discriminately is to be like a man who sells his muscle because he is hungry.

Africa's estimated coal reserves can last for another 300 years. Petroleum fields are being discovered every year to increase Africa's power potential; solar energy is merchantable and Africa has uranium for nuclear energy. But in spite of the fact that the continent possesses industrial raw materials and abundant power and energy, Africa is the least industrialized continent. This is the truth about Africa: It has everything, and yet possesses nothing.

Yes at independence, Africa was given the national anthem, the flag, the twenty-one gun salute and the governors' residence. Nothing changed. A model of Westminster and Whitehall remained in operation; yet that was a solemn moment, a moment of thought and not jubilation, a moment to consider the meaning and problems of statecraft, a moment to discover the philosophic and eternal meaning of the state as a concept. Africa had, at that moment, an opportunity to eclipse the colonial experience and drag the African countries through the usual course of history - injustice, class-war revolution and destruction. Africa chose the latter. African leaders squandered the reserves left by the colonialists' governments, like prodigal sons and took the begging-bowl around, to the same colonial masters, forgetting that even in those seemingly adverse conditions we were part of the most richly endowed continent on the face of the planet.

It is often said that the enemy of African development is neo-colonialism. This is false. Neocolonialism is the advantage, which the strong nations have over the weak ones: it is a law of life. "… to him that hath, shall more be given and from him that hath not, shall be taken away even that which he hath".

Europe is in danger of American domination; Asia is in danger of Chinese and Japanese domination; South America is in danger of North American domination and Africa, the weakest of all continents is in danger of domination by all of them.

The truth is that no one can teach his competitors against himself. Colonial countries cannot teach us how to compete successfully with them; they cannot teach us how to exploit our natural resources to our advantage. They must rather take advantage of our ignorance in order to survive.

It is generally observed that nations emerging from long foreign domination generally lacked an independent administrative traditional social structure within which it was easy to build a class of national administrators. It is true that in some of the countries concerned, the former administering authority had bequeathed a valuable legacy in the form of an efficient administrative apparatus and sizeable cadres of experienced local officials at many levels. But this by no means was generally so. Even where it was, it did not meet the needs of people whose awakening had stirred much deeper feelings of hope and endeavor than were felt under the most enlightened colonial regime.

Having been into the world characterized by an almost unshakable belief in economic growth and progress, Africa's first steps towards `Uhuru' were inevitably influenced by the spirit of development that had seized the rest of the world. Compared to Asia and Latin America, Africa was viewed as having a special opportunity of making rapid and steady progress because it lacked the oppressive social structures and cultural impediments believed to exist on the other two continents. Alas, the reverse is true.

In this climate, the temptation for African leaders to ignore the past and treat their societies as clean slates' was understandably great. Often trained in Universities in the metropolitan of the colonial countries, they wanted their countries to catch up with the rest of the world as quickly as possible and without the pains and strains that had accompanied the march to progress elsewhere. Against this background, it is therefore not surprising that the first decades of independence have been a period of endless imitation and experimentation. Applying pet notions from both East and West with the view to bringing Africa into the mainstream of economic development, the continent was treated much like an empty box.

The time span of a generation later, it is now clear that it was an imaginary expectation that the transfer of power from imperialist countries to sovereign African States would usher in a new era and lead to an improvement in the living standards of the majority of the people. Progress in the sense outlined above, has been much harder to achieve than was held more than sixty years ago and today, Africa is faced with a steady increasing mal-development i.e. with costly legacies of the efforts to find shortcuts to progress! Rather than being closer to the industrialized countries Africa is farther away, rather than being more self-reliant, it is more dependent and rather than being more stable the continent is more volatile and conflict-ridden. In fact, in most countries in Africa the situation has deteriorated even much farther, famine disease and civil wars resulting in an alarming loss of human life and total abuse of human rights with a complete disregard for the sanctity of human life, replacing other historically entrenched stereotypes. Indeed the prevailing image of Africa is that of a continent in permanent need of assistance and salvation from outside; the African having been reduced to a level of consumer apprentices incapable of analyzing their own problems or becoming the protagonists of their own development.

The shortcomings in economic and social performance in Africa over the past decades are the results not only of the misconception of development indicated earlier in this analysis but also symptomatic of an institutional crisis which has not been given the attention it deserves. Public sector institutions created in the optimistic years after independence have found difficulty in adapting to a situation requiring restrain and belt tightening. This problem is particularly pertinent in Africa because of the dominant position taken by the state in development and the weakness of the other institutions in society.

The state-centered approach is at least in part a colonial legacy. Created quite arbitrarily by the colonial powers to respond to their own interests the modern state in Africa was set up with little or no regard for the ethnic linguistic, economic or geographical features of the continent. Nor

was it created with a view to encouraging peoples'
participation in the economic and political business of
their countries. A class of colonial civil servants-
controlled development in the colonial set up. For
reasons of political control, the colonial authorities were
reluctant to promote the establishment of associations
outside the immediate tutelage of the colonial state.

Ironically, independent Africa inherited this legacy.
Initially, as long as government involvement in public
affairs and development was relatively limited, the
problem was manageable. But, as the demand for social
change accelerated, and foreign donors increased their
contributions, state participation in development grew
rapidly and, in some cases, indiscriminately. The
weaknesses of the private and voluntary sectors were
used as an excuse for the rapid growth of state
involvement in both social and economic development.
There was a strong and erroneous belief that through
manpower development programs, institutional
shortcomings could be overcome. However, today, it is
increasingly clear that Africa's problem is not primarily
lack of talent and know-how but the institutional
imbalance created in decades past, both prior to and after
independence. In fact, the excessive reliance on the state
as the principal mechanism of change and development
has left most African countries in a corner from which
they have great difficulties extricating themselves.

The combination of artificiality and predominance has placed great strains on governance. Although an African state was a judicial reality in international law, it was not necessarily at the time of independence an empirical reality in national fact. Independence therefore, opened a gap between the international legitimacy and the internal marginality of many emergent African states. The gap often presented a real political dilemma to the new African leaders. They usually could retain European officials only by compromising their national independence and could dispose with them only at the risk of undermining government performance. Because of the fragile empirical reality of African states, power also tended to become highly personalized.

Against this background, it is not surprising that the greatest threats to political stability in Africa have come from internal rather than external forces, which is not to deny that external forces have played and continue to play a sinister role in the power politics of many African countries. Illustrations of this whole problem is the fact that there have been over 150 attempts to overthrow incumbent governments by force in Africa since 1960 and a good number of them have been successful. An important reason for this is that personalization and monopolization of power stemming from the empirical predicament of African statehood, has limited the scope of power sharing and this drives opponent of incumbent rulers to use force.

Fortunately, the African Union no longer give recognition to any military government in Africa.

 The struggle of the African people for independence was accompanied by many a protestation of anti-imperialism. Even now, many African leaders articulate anti-imperialist slogans while collaborating with the same imperialists against the real interests of the people. This is because nothing in substance has changed. It is high time that anti-imperialism was given a concrete content in the examination of the crisis in Africa. What is the role of imperialism in the era of an African independent state? How does imperialism operate in the conditions of political organizations like the AU and regional economic grouping like ECOWAS, COMESA, SADC etc? How do international finance agencies such as the IMF, World Bank etc, serve the interests of imperialism and how can this be countered? The next chapter seeks answers to these questions.

CHAPTER TWO
PROBLEM OF THE INHERITED STATE

The problem in Africa is largely an institutional one. In particular, it is a problem of the state. The dilemma facing the African State is that because it was inherited, in many instances, just like an empty shell, from the colonial powers, the African leaders, in filling this lacuna, have devoted prime attention to defining and redefining power relations within their societies. They are at the same time being asked to implement, often ill-conceived and usually donor funded development programs and projects with unrealistic time horizons. It is therefore not surprising that in this situation short-term considerations have taken precedence over long-term ones; power over welfare; personal over institutional considerations and security over development. But in a situation where not only human welfare, but also human life is increasingly at stake in the continent, how much longer can Africa afford to be caught in these contradictions. The continent is certainly witnessing an alarming waste of human life and a total abuse of human rights in conflict situations like in the Great Lakes Region, Sudan, Somalia, Ethiopia, Eritrea, Mali and Nigeria. Indeed, millions of precious lives have been callously wasted in Burundi, Rwanda, The Democratic Republic of Congo, Angola, Liberia and

Sierra Leon. What are the options of getting out of this present predicament? How can African statehood be enhanced and development accelerated in a parallel fashion?

These are the questions that are increasingly pre-occupying the minds of progressive - thinking policy makers in and outside Africa. In fact, one should not lose sight of the machinations of the western world in the problem in Africa. Africa's attempt at economic and political groupings has been very disquieting to the U.S.A and Europe. The extent of the West's economic interests in Africa is not a secret. A scientific analysis of the African continent should look beyond empirical data to discover the forces that sustain and nurture political instability and economic stagnation in Africa. Why does the U.S.A find itself so much involved in the affairs not only of some African countries but also of South East Asia, the Middle East and other areas where European countries prior to World War 11 were predominant? An analysis of the structure of world economy will reveal the relative position of states and their role today in the global world economy that has led to the problems of development in Africa.

There is no doubt, whatsoever, that between Britain, the United States, France, West Germany, Canada and Japan, there exists a complete network of horizontal and vertical network and ties expressing the fact that individual

national economies ultimately become links in the western economies. In these economies, each economic unit plays an assigned role in the international division of labor. Historically the position occupied by a particular country in the imperialist chain changed as a result of:
a) world war
b) changes in financial resources,
c) the correlation of classes and class struggle within each country.

When Britain was the leading imperialist country, she was also the main beneficiary of the world economy.

After World War 11 when the fortunes of British imperialism began to decline, the United States saw itself (especially in relation to British dominions) as the heir apparent and political Centre of the English speaking world. After World War II the U. S. carried its imperialist aims both against and in cooperation with Europe colonial powers and especially in collaboration with Britain and through the latter's agency. But for Britain and Europe, this collaboration was merely expressive of their own decline as world powers and in which their dependence on the U.S.A. was revealed. Under imperialism economic annexation of one country by another was fully achievable without political annexation. This fact must be born in mind in analyzing the changes in the role of particular countries in the present historical epoch. It makes it possible to understand the ascendancy of U.S. imperialism in the course of the breakup of the old colonial systems - a fact African leaders failed to understand in their post independent relations with the Western world. The penetration of US capital in the various regions of the world is one of the prime economic foundations of the US ascendancy. The strategic aim of the US capital investments after the breakup of formal colonialism was/is to keep countries within the bounds of the capitalist world economy strongly controlled by the US. It is therefore not surprising that the US and the European countries, particularly Britain under the Conservative government led by Margaret Thatcher tirelessly worked towards the total eclipse of the communist world. In fact the emergence of African continental and regional groupings which are striving to link both political with economic independence has greatly aggravated the U.S and its allies problems of economic control in Africa. But what are the options for getting out of this present predicament? This is the question that needs answers from an African point of view. The Lagos Plan of Action, subsequent statements adopted by African Heads of State (including the African Priority Program for Economic Recovery), and NEPAD were indicative of this concern at governmental levels in Africa. They also featured on the agenda of the growing community of non-governmental organizations, African or international, involved in African development matters. Even certain genuine donor agencies were taking a serious look at what they had been doing for Africa.

While all these efforts seemed encouraging, it was not clear whether the full dimensions of the African problems were realized. There was still a widely held belief that with more money and better technology, Africa's problems will be solved. Surely, such a `business as usual' recipe was the surest road to disaster at a time when old relations between ends and means did not hold; action frustrates its own intentions; and new purposes flounder for want of understanding and knowledge. At the same time, it was clear that it was easy to describe the problems in Africa and preach large changes of heart, yet neither description nor exhortation sufficed at the time. More respect for the African Voice, independent analysis, more frequent dialogue and interaction and an extension of the number of actors involved in thinking and deciding about public matters, are some of the means that need to be considered in the present situation. In short, there must and ought to be greater participation by the broader base of the African people in the political and economic business of their countries.

In analyzing constraints and opportunities in order to resolve the present contradictions in Africa, we have to consider the pre-colonial, colonial and post colonial legacies assuming that each contained elements of significance to the present challenge. We believe that out of this rationale, we can come out with the rationale for a new perspective.

CHAPTER THREE
THE PRE-COLONIAL LEGACY

One of the pernicious effects of colonialism was to implant, notably among the educated Africans, the racist idea that Africa had neither history nor culture, or at best, that if there was one it was of no relevance today. The idea of colonialism as a civilizing mission and the policies of colonial powers pursued were calculated to destroy African resistance and to justify the brutality that would not normally be meted out on human beings.

 While the need to study Africa's history should naturally be motivated by idealism designed to counter colonialist myths by other myths. Such as glorifying everything in Africa's past, it should, however, as in all other countries, be studied and made to serve objectively and subjectively the present and the future of the African continent. On this premise, We hope that our analysis of Africa's pre-colonial institutions will enable us to arrive at a number of useful conclusions.

 Before colonization, African societies were not organized in 'States' in the modern Sense. Centralization of power and bureaucratization - two important attributes of the state - had not developed in Africa or they were only at the most embryonic stages. Some of the reasons for this were:

a) the rarity of writing

b) the non-existence of wheeled vehicles, which by limiting long distance travel, limited centralization

c) the late arrival of firearms which prevented state absolution until recent times d) the absence, in large parts of Africa, of religions with ambitions of Universality and

e) the rarity of unifying language.

This broad generalization of the pre-colonial situation in Africa should not by any means imply that family and kinship systems were the only social and political structures of importance in this period. The development of productive forces and social formations five centuries ago, in key areas such as iron and copper smelting, cloth manufacturing, leather tanning and dying as well as in trade in these items were unevenly distributed across the African continent. In Egypt, Nubia, the Maghreb, Ethiopia, the Western Sudan (comprising Ghana, Mali and Songhai) the inter-lacustrine kingdoms of East Africa and Zimbabwe were elaborate political-military and economic systems, which bore similarities with feudal societies, especially in Asia. These states had developed as early as a thousand years before Africa's permanent contact with Europe. However, quite significantly, the African societies were not given the chance to undergo social revolutions such as those that gave rise to the capitalist revolution in Europe in the 19th century. This was one way Europe underdeveloped Africa.

The fundamental traits that existed in the political life of pre-colonial African societies, which could be emulated, were as follows:

The basic principle in African political life, which was ignored by subsequent colonial systems, was the socialization of political and economic power. In spite of differences between the village community and more centralized kingdoms in West and Central Africa dating back to the 10th Century, this principle prevailed. While social differentials existed within these societies, there were no contradictions, which could not be resolved without the overthrow of one social stratum by another.

Although there were tyrannies and abuses of power in both state-societies and stateless societies during the pre-colonial period, there were also ideal principles, which governed them. Community interests invariably eclipsed individual rights, but there also existed principles and practices for their protection. The situation was more expressive for the women although at the same time, in some parts of Africa, women played important political and military roles. In Egypt, Namibia, Benin, Angola, Ethiopia and Zimbabwe, in different periods, women ruled and produced some of the legendary names in the military history of Africa. Women, religious leaders as well as leaders of secret societies enjoyed privileged

positions which also had political and economic power and led in the feudal period, for example in Ethiopia to the widely held idea of the divineness of the role of the Solomonic line. Nonetheless, the most important postulate of the African exercise of power was the search for an equilibrium between political actors, in essence the application of three great principles;
a a) limitation of power
b b) sharing of power
c) rule of law.

 In order to realize the first principle, power was limited by tradition and custom which also assigned roles, responsibilities and power according to age, place occupied in the production process and social hierarchy. It was also guaranteed by extensive freedom of expression in the context of well-established and scrupulously respected codes. Indeed, it was not only the liberty to speak that was given, it was an obligation to speak on behalf of those ones represented (family, caste or clan). This right of expression was not without its limitations for the ordinary people, but councilors, historians, minstrels and other dignitaries retained full rights to express themselves and their opinions even if these were unpopular and critical of the rulers.

 Yet, another factor limiting power in African society was the disassociation of political power from economic power. In some societies, the Bambara for instance, the political head of a village (teng naba) was different from the soil (economic) chief (teng soba). In Buganda, the 'bataka' clan leaders were the custodians of land for their clansmen, while the kabaka and his chiefs were the political leaders.

The second great principle throughout Africa was power-sharing. It was always believed that the best way to keep power was to share it with as many groups as possible so that each had interest in its preservation. In the Mossi Empire in Mali, for example, the king was elected by an electoral college made up of non-nobles so that they could observe the principle of neutrality between competing members of the nobility. In some countries (Rwanda and Burundi Kingdoms) elaborated legal procedures existed in which ordinary people were chosen to serve as judges, notary public and 'ombudsmen' on the basis of their knowledge of customs and traditions and because of their personal integrity. Armed forces in Africa were only mobilized for action against external enemies, or against rebellions by feudal lords against their kings. Before the 13th century, the professional armies in other countries were first and foremost used for conquest of domestic power rather than for defense from external enemies.

Finally, the African State was governed by the rule of law. Law was prescribed by custom and not even the king was above it. In many African Kingdoms, the king was sub-ordinated to the interest of the people that when he became so old and weak as to be considered harmful to their well-being, he was killed in ritual - a measure which would also be taken in case of gross violations of custom and tradition or in case of treachery. In some societies, the king was merely the representative of the ancestors in whom power resided or the `Stool' descended from heaven which was the real symbol of authority.

It is recognized that the most fundamental reality, from which the present features of the crisis in Africa originate, is the inherited colonial state, its methods of conquests, legitimization and perpetuation in the different phases of colonization. It is further recognized that far from negating the effects of the slave trade, which had existed in Africa from the tenth century onwards, colonization reinforced, in many ways, the important effects of the slave trade, particularly in the formation of primary institutions and their chance of enduring.

From the tenth century to the sixteenth century, Muslim trans-Saharan and Trans-Indian Ocean slave trade had the impact of dislocating the autonomous development of African societies and institutions. Political systems and social traditions which elsewhere in Europe and Asia provided the setting for the development of `high cultures' and which were evident in many societies in Africa were destabilized although they were still evident and could have survived that slave trade. The appearance of European slave traders in the 16th century with more efficient weapons accelerated the pace and enlarged the extent of the slave trade. Even the most conservative estimates of the number of slaves taken from Africa, to which must be added those who died from diseases, wars and famines which accompanied the accursed trade, would still provide sufficient evidence of the devastation by and of the lingering effect of slavery and the slave trade. That most sought-after slaves were those in the prime of their lives, able-bodied men and women, is an often ignored significant fact in considering the demographic and economic consequences of the slave trade. It was indeed a "sin that no saint can ever cleanse".

The destruction by the slave trade of the political and social formations which hitherto had provided protection of the individual led to the reinforcement of dependency on kinship systems and kin groups - the most basic units of social organizations. In most African countries, at the advent of colonization, the kinship system had remained and retained the function of being, in the absence of the state, the most valued social defense of the African individual.

Furthermore, with few exceptions, slavery deprived Africa of the possibility of developing the feudal mode of production which in Europe encouraged political structures and social moves that gave the state power in the defense of individuals against external danger and in reconciling their conflicting interests. Under feudalism submission to legitimate political authorities, and to demands as were made by those authorities, was reinforced by defense and protection of the individual and his property. Rights and duties were established and scrupulously followed and the notion of citizen took root. Systems of demarcation between public and private interests were evolved in the long history of conquests, regrouping and domination; from small territorial units and different ethnic groups to larger and politically and culturally more integrated societies in which traditions of leadership and accountability were perfected and firmly rooted. In Africa, by contrast, colonialism did not integrate different societies into larger and more viable systems. It set out to dominate all of them using as its most effective weapon, the strategy of "divide and rule"

The colonial state distinguished itself by an excessive use of force. Unlike development in Europe, where the state evolved over centuries of colonialism achieved its objective in a very short time because it had monopoly over arms. Acting without any moral restraint in its use of force, the colonial state first made war on society and thereafter used the same instruments of war to keep society under its domination.

The response by Africans, which also suited the colonial order, was the withdrawal even more deeply into pre-colonial kinship systems in which the individual was protected and fulfilled, and which he/she gave total allegiance. At the same time, being so weakened, these systems could not individually and separately pose any threat to the colonial order. These factors of the colonial state gave rise to the following phenomena:

■ State and society were set apart as were their interests.

■ The state did not exist in the context of the morality of the African society at was therefore not responsible to it.

■ The state was essentially in a permanent situation of war with society, which in turn was in a situation of permanent resistance.

■ Being amoral, the colonial state would only be dealt with amorally by the society. Thus individual and collective behavior internalized these features and relations between the colonial state and society.

The state -society relations which developed out of the slave trade and colonialism engendered two realms in constant conflict: an amoral and ill-conceived civic realm on one hand and a circumscribed community-based on moral realm on the other. Attitudes towards organization, management and control of public affairs and resources reflected, and continue to reflect this basic divergence of interests of state and society. Embezzlement of public funds and disregard for public property including nepotism and other forms of corruption must be understood in part as the defense of self and immediate family/clan against the state. By the same token family, clan or ethnic group will tax itself severely and willingly because the taxes go into a common pot for the benefit of all. In contrast, the colonial state did not take into consideration the interests of the society. In its exploitation of labor, for example, it paid such low wages that the laborers had to fall back on their families for their livelihood on returning from mines and plantations where they were employed. In the final analysis, the labor demanded of the head of the family was to enable him to pay the head tax in return for the individual's freedom and that of the family. Failure to pay tax made him a real prisoner or permanent fugitive in hiding from the agents of the state. Taxes were therefore considered a punishment rather than a duty conferring on the tax payer entitlement to social benefits, human and political rights in a free society. Payment of tax did not give the payer the right to question the reason and manner in which the taxes would be dispensed, reinforcing even further the non-accountability of the state to the individual.

One important question, as we examine the first problem in Africa, in the Congo, Lumumba's dilemma in 1960 is, can real liberation be carried out within the framework of the colonial state? The question is predicated on the fact that the post colonial state carries most of, if not, all the features of the colonial state and is perceived by the citizenry to be performing the same role with more or less perfected instruments and structures.

CHAPTER FOUR
THE POST-COLONIAL LEGACY

History matters in the study of change. The path taken in the past can eliminate options, because of inherited structures, institutions, ideologies, attitudes, and values (including *apartheid*, colonialism, and nationalism).
The relatively peaceful decolonization of British and French Africa in the 1950s and 1960s led, for the most part, to the capturing of state power by a new political elite rather than a thorough-going transformation of the state structures inherited at independence. Instead of refashioning institutions in ways that might increase political participation and social justice, existing state capacities tended to be marshaled for exclusionary and, in many cases, authoritarian purposes.

Countries like the former Portuguese colonies, Zimbabwe, Namibia and South Africa however, did not follow this model of consensual decolonization. There, entrenched settler regimes had no intention of voluntarily liquidating their control and were prepared to resist indefinitely the move toward decolonization. Settler intransigence forced African opposition underground and set in motion what was to become protracted liberation struggles. Unprecedented political changes forged in the heat of armed struggle, it is claimed, irreversibly supposed to determine the character of the coming state. The imperatives of mobilizing against a recalcitrant colonialism, inevitably involved a basic reordering of social relationships. According to Basil Davidson, popular organization and the creation of an alternative politics meant that the new rulers would have 'no need to take over any of the structures and institutions of colonial rule' (Davidson1976:75). And for Patrick Cabal, 'successful people's wars usher in the establishment of states the legitimacy and structure of which owe little, if anything to their colonial predecessors (Chabal, 1983:218)).

According to the mobilization thesis, the character of the post-colonial state in these societies would have an 'inevitable' and positive connection to the insurgent 'state' that was built up in liberated zones during the struggle for independence. Since the years of liberation struggle produced a political culture and practice in opposition to the colonial system, it was expected that a revolutionary, seemingly irrevocable break had to be accomplished.

However, we must never forget that the settler colonial state in these countries was an authoritarian bureaucratic apparatus of control and not intended to be a school of democracy. Its European officials believed themselves to be agents of a superior civilization with a right to rule

over people of inferior culture and paternally guide them
to a higher level of social development. However
haphazard and ramshackle the reality of state power, the
settler colonialists struggled to maintain the façade of
omnipotence and omniscience. Their sense of being a
legitimate and uniquely capable ruling class was passed on
through the elite secondary schools and, eventually,
universities that trained cadres of potential African
successors to run not only the former capitalist
enterprises, but also the apparatus of the bureaucratic
state. It is therefore not surprising that, since
independence, the new governments' institutions and
structures in almost every African country display a
striking degree of continuity with its colonial predecessor.
 Institutions and Structures of governance took the
pattern of the settler colonial regimes, with executive,
legislature, and judiciary as the main pillars of
government, supplemented by an elaborate civil
service/public sector and other government and semi-
government agencies.

Thus, Africa's struggle for independence was the
outcome of contradictions inherent in the colonial system
itself. Having secured territorial boundaries and control
of the population, the administration of the state and the
organization of production imposed the need to train a
small fraction of indigenous people to perform
supporting roles. Education was the vehicle through
which the state indoctrinated the African colonial

servants into accepting as unquestionable the imperatives of the colonial state, essentially autonomy and hegemony, inviolability and security of territory, in spite of the arbitrariness of the colonial boundaries and diversity of the population.

Where the pre-colonial African society had already advanced towards clearly defined social class formations and, in particular, where the model of production and social relations had created ruling families/clans, the colonial state instituted `indirect rule', in order to use them as intermediary class between the state and the people. The sons and daughters of the chiefs, and chiefly clans, religious converts and traders were consequently educated into accepting the basic ideology of the colonial state.

In order to understand the nature of the post-colonial state, it is important to look into the condition of the class that led the nationalist independence movement and see, whether, given the circumstances that had nurtured it, it could bring about the results which the people expected once it took over power from the colonialist.

In the chapter on the pitfalls of National consciousness Frantz Fanon in 'THE WRETCHED OF THE EARTH' made the sharpest critique of the African Middle Classes which led the independence movements and were the architects of the postcolonial state. "The educated middle classes as already observed, were drawn from traditional ruling families, land owners, merchants and traders and those who accepted conversion to the religion of the colonizing power. These latter were sent to mission schools where they were taught not only to give God his due, but Caesar as well in proportions set by the missions and the colonial state respectively. Through the education they received and the place they occupied in the colonial state administration the mostly non-productive role in the economy and its appetite for European goods and culture, the African middle classes lost all but the most superficial links with the people. In the name of the people the middle classes agitated for independence without any concrete notion of what that independence meant for the people".

The middle classes - the petit bourgeoisie - were only certain of their immediate interests, which were not different from those of the colonial state agents. Abolition of the most naked abuses of the colonial state - inequality of remuneration between equally trained African and European technicians, forced labor, disenfranchisement and racial discrimination in social intercourse, constituted for the petit bourgeoisie the most urgent task of the independence movement. For example the ANC of Southern Rhodesia, as quoted in Bowman, declared its aims and objectives as "primarily dedicated to a political program, economic and educational advancement, social service and personal standards. Its aim is the national unity of all inhabitants of the country in true partnership regardless of race, color and creed congress affirms complete loyalty to the crown as the symbol of national unity. It is not a racial movement. It is equally opposed to racialism and tribalism … congress believes that individual initiative and free enterprise are necessary to the life of a young country and must be fully encouraged, but that a considerable measure of government control is necessary in a modern state …this country greatly needs capital from overseas … (and) government must therefore establish conditions under which capital may be invested and industry established with sufficient security to encourage investors".

Being numerically small and struggling against western colonial systems which originated from countries practicing bourgeoisie democracy, it was necessary for the middle class to seek the following of the majority of the people so as to swell their numbers, and to make it impossible for the colonial state to govern.

Such mass following was also important in mobilizing international public opinion and especially the opinion of the liberals in the metropolitan countries, where their pressure would play an important role in the decolonization process. Therefore, unity among the people and submerging all class and ethnic differences was of the utmost strategic significance.

In summary, the class that took over the state on being granted independence by the metropolitan country saw as its mission the replacement of foreign rule by African rule. Approaching the question of exploitation from a racial perspective, the nationalist government leaders legitimized local exploitation carried out by its supporters as 'fruits of independence,' and explained away the increasing misery of its people resulting from, among other things, iniquitous laws of the international economic order about which they could do nothing.

Moreover, the African post-colonial state was exposed to two international political models - the Westminster parliamentary democracy and the Stalinist one-party absolutism. Neither of these was particularly relevant to Africa and increasingly criticized in their respective countries of origin. Trying to make sense of these models, African leaders turned democracy into personality cults, factors that invariably contributed to the phenomenon of the coup d'éta

Not surprising the coup makers always promised to honor international agreements entered into by the overthrown governments. These promises were made basically in order to assure the transnational corporations and other foreign capitalists that their interest would not be touched. The promises made to the people on the other hand were seldom kept. The people who always rose in support of the coup-any coup-soon found out the true colors of the coup makers. The state was hardly ever affected by the coup. When coup attempt failed, mass

arrests, imprisonment and firing squads became the lot of those caught and those suspected of complicity.
Successful coups usually led to even worse orders. Not having any roots among the people, the only way the new regimes could survive was through suppression of the people and physical liquidation of real and imaginary enemies.

Even where scientific methods and modes were claimed, the exhortations and left-wing slogans were only designed to conceal the wishes of the state for unquestionable compliance from the people. Even when the state came about as a result of armed struggle like in Angola, Algeria, Mozambique and Zimbabwe, in which tremendous sacrifices were made by the fighters and the entire population, the situation was no better than in those countries where it came about through some peace. It was more disappointing as expectations were high, that in those states greater identification of the state and people would be painstakingly nurtured and that out of experiences of the savage wars of liberation, the state would not betray the people's confidence.

The unity that was the liberation movement's strongest weapon against the colonial power, however, did not take long to erode once independence was achieved. What were claimed as ideological differences among the leadership were often smoke screens for imperialist forces to divide the people so that it would appear as if they were struggles for power attributed to lack of democracy in the African state. Indeed, there developed some internal conflicts within the leadership which resulted in less and less attention being paid to real issues. Contact with the people was gradually lost.

Also, the post-colonial legacy is replete with examples of states' perspectives on problems being too often dictated by one leader of groups of state supported intellectuals who behave and act as if their ideas are valid. Because these perspectives are not debated by the people, or at best only superficially explained, they lack practicability and are almost invariably the cause of great waste of resources, suffering and despair. It is increasingly evident that policies are being determined solely by concern with the means rather than conditions of development. The former has given rise to preoccupation with structures leading to centralization and expansion of the state beneficiaries and has strongly encouraged a top-bottom approach to management of public affairs. This has resulted in preventing the majority of the peoples of Africa from active participation in the political, economic, social and cultural business of their various countries. The leaders of the mass movements, which brought about legal independence in Africa, inherited the totality of the colonial state they had been fighting against. Lowering the 'Union Jack' or the 'Tricolor', African Heads of State moving to former governors' residences (thereafter renamed 'Peoples' Palace or State House), the twenty-one-gun salute or the national anthem, did not signify any basic change. Rather than question its relevance, the colonial state was adopted and legitimized. As a matter of fact, far from bringing the promised salvation to the people of Africa, the African leaders sunk deep into the love for flashy scenes and high faulting words. More important is the historical fact that in a very radical sense the nationalist leaders of Africa have found themselves sucked into the role of hypocrites and actors involved in a make-belief situation.

Whereas bureaucracy had run the colonial state, the emergent African State lacked the administrative structures, personnel and the culture necessary for the efficient management and organization of state and society with different objectives from those of the colonial state. 'STATIZATION' of all aspects of the economic social and cultural life of the people which necessitated the expansion of the bureaucracy was the response of the post-colonial African states. It however did not increase efficiency. On the contrary, it became a burden to society as more and more resources were required to maintain it. The African state not only became the principal industry, it also sought and succeeded in interfering in the most personal and private lives of its citizens. The African state developed fastest in setting up capacities for repression and in systematically attempting to control and to organize society and individuals so as to gain their unquestioning allegiance.

Indeed revolutionary fervor gutted into political betrayal. Personal liberties were severely eroded.

It is because of these policies of African States in the last sixty years that the masses of African people have witnessed political and economic stagnation, mass starvation, wars, torture and other forms of repression. Most of these are traceable to the state by the internal and external policies it pursued or by its inaction where intervention was required.

Africa has learnt through great pains that the content of independence lay not in the seizing of power from the colonialist, but in how and for what that power was exercised. At the time of independence, African household by and large could feed themselves. The African continent was not the major recipient of food aid than it has become, and its prospects for development were as less evident than in countries of Asia, which had been under the same colonial empires.

The political crisis beginning with the Congo in 1960 multiplied in the sixties and seventies. These crises were to result in Africa's inability to organize internal political and economic policies, which would make them economically self-sufficient and independent actors in the community of nations.

As the crisis deepened, so did theories to explain its origin, nature and magnitude and to propose 'appropriate' paths to development. Various schools of thought sprang up and many theories were advanced to explain Africa's underdevelopment. Too often African policy-makers accepted lock, stock and barrel, these theories without questioning their reliability even when their own empirical experiences were enough to expose the inadequacy of these theories most of which are mainly western and form part of aid packages which have become the intellectual mentors of these African policy-makers.

One of the theories propounded is the one termed 'development studies'. Development studies is itself in a crisis because from its inception, after the Second World War, as a branch of economics, not a single country can be shown to have developed on any of the numerous models it has produced. On the contrary, development studies has itself become another opium for the people, designed, (as they often were), to stop the peoples of Africa, Asia and Latin America from objectively investigating the real causes of their underdevelopment. At the same time, the establishment of multilateral institutions like the IBRD, the IMF, the OECD and the EU pursue a strategy, which opens up the African economies to further penetration through erroneously much sought after foreign investments. In reality Foreign Direct Investment (FDI) means further economic exploitation.

In fact, we believe that the problem in Africa is not only about balance of payment and inadequate or misdirected external aid. The political and social upheavals, intensive wars, the enormous Africa refugee problem, extensive migration of African laborers within and outside Africa encompass broader moral and political issues.

Understanding of the root causes of Africa's underdevelopment, namely European Capitalism, through its slave, colonial and neo-colonial phases, while being necessary in raising the consciousness of the people, is too often used by the state intellectual apologists, to exculpate themselves from the responsibility of conceptualizing new paradigms within which the people could be mobilized to make their own history. For much too long, Africa's intellectuals in their typically middle-class superficiality, have harped on everything negative in the political, social and cultural life of Africa as being the result of external pressures or constraints. By so proselytizing, the implication is that the correction of these wrongs will also have to come from outside.

More than fifty five years of independence have given Africans rich experiences, even if, for the most part, they were of a negative character. They, however, provide a platform for an in-depth process of thought and action, geared towards the creation of a new domestic order that is culturally relevant, morally justifiable, economically vibrant and politically geared towards real liberation. That process can only be meaningful if it starts with inward looking consciousness.

Although there has been much talk about self reliance and integrated development since African countries became independent, little has been done to foster a process that builds on local resources and serves to integrate sectoral efforts. Africa has remained standing with its back to its hinterland. We would certainly like to stress that the economic crisis in the past few years provides an unusual opportunity for rethinking and reorganizing the continent's economies. To be sure, the economic performance of African countries has varied and some are better off than others are. The truth of the matter is that every African country shares a debt burden and unfavorable terms of trade that gives them little choice but to reconsider past policies. African government leaders must, therefore, discover the potential of the domestic economy and society. Donors and other international organizations must adjust their approach to Africa in such a way that local initiatives are encouraged, local know-how tapped, and local institutions developed as counter-measures to the overwhelming legacy of externally induced and controlled interventions, whether by public or private institutions.

The existing production structures reflect the colonial

priorities: production of raw materials and other commodities in demand in Europe and other industrialized countries. The result is that African countries tend to produce similar products, compete for the same market and often end up experiencing depressing terms of trade to their own disadvantage. Again, because African economies are essentially non-complementary, there is only limited scope for intra African trade, in spite of the political rhetoric to the contrary. African countries continue to produce what they do not consume and consume what they do not produce. The end result of that is that they are extremely exposed to changes in the international market prices and other external variables. In the 1990s in particular, commodity prices have been generally low while prices on imports, especially for the manufacturing sector, have gone up. The inevitable outcome has been escalating debts. While these debts in absolute terms may at first glance appear modest, they constitute heavy burdens. Foreign debt service makes up several percent of the gross domestic product (GDP) and, an average in sub-Saharan Africa, over a quarter of export earnings.

 A precondition for autonomous and integrated development is that people rely on their own diligent labor, behave frugally and invest in the creation of new productive resources rather than consuming and dissipating capital produced. Productive activities must also be better linked to each other, whether forward or backward. For instance, enhanced food production, production of clothing material and clothes, as well as the provision of better housing will strengthen the domestic market. This process is likely to take time to realize but it should be given priority as a means of reducing export dependency and vulnerability to changes in the global economy. By building a strategy of industrialization on the agricultural sector, greater complimentarily between rural and urban-based production can be achieved. This principle can also be applied in regional African contexts. Investment has to be rationalized and made to serve more than one country. Food banks and other strategic institutions for inter-state transfers should be seriously considered.

CHAPTER FIVE
GREATER AFRICAN EFFECTIVE PARTICIPATION IN THE INTERNATIONAL FORUM

Although African countries are weak by comparison with most other countries, there is great need for taking the necessary action to assert their position more forcefully in international fora. It is a matter of:
(1) developing common positions on key issues;
(2) enhancing analytical skills; and
(3) strengthening negotiating abilities.
For instance, what would happen if the African governments jointly developed a carefully prepared position on what to do with the continents' debilitating external debt?

There are several constraints to effective action on this issue but most of them lie within the realm of what can be overcome. This analysis identify the following:
(1) Poor selection of delegates to important conferences;
(2) Inadequate negotiating skills and
(3) Lack of training and experience in substantial fields.

Selection of delegates, particularly to international conferences, are often made as a reward for political work or as a means of providing an occasion for vacationing. Lack of individuals with negotiating skills is another constraint. African negotiators did very well in the constitutional conferences preceding independence. Why is the continent so short of skilled negotiators today? One explanation is that there is a shortage of competent individuals with adequate experience in a given field. The political emphasis in the past three decades has been to produce generalists rather than specialists. It is therefore not surprising that African countries have often failed to put up the necessary competence and know-how to serve official negotiators in various international fora.

The principal means to change that this analysis identifies is intra-African cooperation. Speaking with one voice on key issues of common concern needs to be further encouraged and so do greater cooperation aimed at fostering a sense of commonness. For instance, in the early sixties, Kenyans, Ugandans and Tanzanians were first and foremost East Africans.

Today the East African is an endangered species' and it requires a reserved commitment and a new perspective to restore such an orientation.

Observation is that most African countries have become addicted to foreign aid, have lost a sensible perspective on what it can, and should do, and that, as a result, foreign aid must be treated as much as part of the problem as part of the solution to Africa's current development crisis. The besieged nature of the African State has recurrently been reinforced by the international donor community through interventions that have often been ill conceived, poorly designed, and inadequately executed. Africa, therefore, needs a greater independence from the donor community. It needs to put its foot down and accept that the answers to Africa's problems lie with the Africans themselves, including those many individuals and groups that are not part of government structures, and not with the donors, however much expertise they might be able to mobilize in their support.

Africans have been brought up worshipping all things foreign. This colonial - or neocolonial mentality is deeply engrained in the African mind. The lack of public debate about who the Africans are, or 'who we are' and 'how to get there' further foster this dependency mentality. The absence of an intellectual atmosphere for discussion of issues of national concern tends to reduce the African to a subservient being, always anxious to take the easy road.

Awareness of the need to develop an independent mind and a new social consciousness that stresses self-reliance will only be achieved through greater respect for intellectual work. Culture has vanished as a significant variable in Africa because of the emphasis by foreign donors on achieving `development' (measured in tangible material terms). Political slogans and foolish ideas must be allowed to give way to more serious research and more critical debate of issues that affect Africa's present and future.

We recognized that the besieged nature of the African State also stems from its inherited colonial boundaries. The latter has become taboo to touch. Much effort and much money been devoted to defending them, although they are too many African boundaries artificially and arbitrary. Nobody was ready to suggest that the official OAU position on the sanctity of the present territorial boundaries should be changed. Whatever is the case, still emphasize the need to form greater respect for cultural and social diversity within these boundaries. Uniformity is not necessarily the same as strength. However, it should also be mentioned that African nations are facing certain dangers in changing to the idea of single nation sovereignty in a world where the increasing power of the European Union and other regional organizations tend to make this idea old fashioned.

The multiplicity of ethnic, racial and religious groups in African countries poses a special challenge. In colonial days, it was tackled by using the principle of 'divide and rule'. Although African leaders usually do it in the name of 'national unity' they very much follow the same principle of divide and rule. The artificiality of the boarders is often used to clamp down on groups that wish to assert their cultural identity.

Greater respect for sub-nationalists and other minorities within each African State should be scrupulously developed so that national unity ceases to be a pretext for prosecution of those who want to protect their rights. Border issues can be settled more amicably and at a less cost to Africa if special efforts are made to develop a political climate in which inter-state action can be promoted. African countries do not have the military resources to resolve or monitor inter-state conflicts, but they can take the necessary political and diplomatic steps to ensure that risk for such conflicts is minimized. Prevention is usually better than cure.

It is observed that at the time of independence and in the years immediately thereafter, the emphasis on national consensus was understandable. Building the new state encouraged such an outlook. Experience has, however, shown that ambition to achieve maximum consensus often backfires. People are alienated underground opposition is encouraged and, political instability, often violence becomes the end result. The political formula adopted at independence, therefore, has become an albatross around Africa's neck. Instead of serving as an engine for propelling growth, the state has become one of the greatest obstacle to progress in Africa. The notion of limitation of power, however, is not new to Africans. It was practiced in pre-colonial societies as indicated earlier in this analysis. Many of these values have survived at the level of local governance. The new perspective called for in this analysis involves these customary African values and principles and emphasizes the need for establishing a state that reflects local standards of fairness and dignity in a dynamic context. Sometimes these standards may coincide with universal values, at other times they may not. The point is that there must be an opportunity for ventilating the question of what is right and wrong, fair and to whom.

On both colonial and post-colonial years, African countries have got used to the practice of 'unlimited government,' i.e. the use of power without any forms of restraint whatsoever. The result has been that most individual people in African countries are intimidated. The emphasis on the state as the principal actor in development has further reinforced an attitude of apathy. People simply sit back and do not engage in civic affairs. Africa has indeed become a continent without participation, although nowhere has the concept been more widely embraced by political leaders. Instead of using 'voice' option and register their opinion, people prefer to use their 'exit' option, i.e. to withdraw from public affairs.

We confirmed in our opinion that the sovereignty of people (society) over the state must be established. This can only happen through the introduction of more democratic practices. Periodic election to a national assembly of contestants picked by committees of the ruling party must give way to multiparty democracy permitting all patriotic parties to freely organize and participate in free and fair elections at all levels of representation. The most crucial level, because it is close to the people, is the village community. If the representative to the district level assembly are elected from the village councils, which in turn are elected directly by the people from among trustworthy honest and respected individuals, political representation will begin to take on a different character. Patronage politics will give way to open democratic practices. Another important measure to limit power and give meaning to democracy among the people is the right to recall representatives when they are deemed to have abused their mandate. If politicians who seek office only for their own enrichment and aggrandizement can get away with it, people will have no trust in the political system. If on the other hand, these politicians who seek office are under pressure by those people who elected them, greater accountability will develop. Finally, I must emphasize the need and the right to form and operate associations whether religious, cultural or professional, with a view to participating in public affairs openly. The rights of assembly, press, speech, etc. have not been respected in Africa. Non-governmental organizations should be strengthened, as development is too important a matter to be left in the hands of a few politicians and government officials only. `The Spirit is too great for one head' if we may cite an African proverb.

A collateral to the need for limiting power of government leaders is the importance of making arrangements for greater sharing of it. The African State has remained set apart from society after independence because of excessive concentration of power in the hands of a small group of people drawn from a ruling political party the civil or military service

The principle constraints are related to the legacies inherited from years of over-centralized and over-politicized rule. These legacies encourage the notion that politics is just another lucrative profession - in some countries perhaps the most lucrative and make individuals regard it merely from the stand point of their own interests. The interests of either the state or the society at large are ignored. Sycophancy, corruption, nepotism and other ills in the African State systems are bred in this climate

Decentralization and de-bureaucratization are essential means to change the present situation. By decentralization is not meant the transfer of power to levels of a culturally controlled government. Such an exercise, as experienced in many African countries only multiplies bureaucratic structures. It enhances state capacity for oppression. Decentralization, therefore, must in the future entail strengthening various forms of local government as well as non-governmental organizations. Only by reducing the stake at each level and in every public institution, will there be a way of bringing about greater democracy.

Fed up by the abuse of power in so many African States, I would like to register the need for greater emphasis on the rule of law. Desirable leadership behavior will not come about voluntarily. Thus, those institutions that enforce the laws of the land must be strengthened. No individual, including the head of state, should be above the law. While I recognize that strengthening the rule of law is a complicated and sensitive process, I would like to emphasize that there is a limit to what individuals living in societies where that principle is ignored, can take. Thus every African must work hard to ensure that political and civil liberties are not arbitrarily ignored by politicians, bureaucrats or others power and influence.

The tragedy of Africa is that the way political systems have been run since independence has led to the institutionalization of a pattern of behavior among leaders that goes contrary to the notion of the rule of law. Politicians almost invariably see themselves as being above the law and are ready to violate laws in order to protect their own interests or persecute somebody challenging their position. The result is that the secret police, sometimes also the army, has become a major instrument of central and defense of the state against real or imaginary enemies. Trials, particularly of political challengers, have usually made a mockery of law.

Limiting the time in office is one way of creating greater opportunity for holding politicians accountable. Promoting peoples' self-confidence through civic education and involvement in public affairs will enhance their ability to resist the tendency towards the rule of individuals rather than the rule of law. A special challenge in many African countries will be the demystification of the gun, i. e. the development of the conditions under which the gun, and other means of state coercion, will be employed responsibly and in the name of protecting the law only. Finally, as part of this process, authorities must be made to show much greater respect for the sanctity of human life and property than has been the case to date. This will come about only if there are constitutional means to hold people in power accountable. The opportunity to express a vote of no confidence in an individual leader in circumstances when that person has violated the law is one possibility.

Respect for private property may be a prerequisite for greater respect for public property. Based on Africa's disappointing experience of nationalization and management of the public sector, we would like to suggest that at the present stage of development in Africa, a better balance between private and public ownership of the means of production, distribution and exchange is needed. Problems to date have been caused not only by lack of skilled manpower, but above all, by lack of responsibility towards public property among stage managers.

The result has been a catastrophe for Africa: loss of the potential for accumulation and reinvestment; destruction of already acquired capital – e.g. machinery, vehicles and equipment – underproduction of consumer goods and therefore hardships for the people and loss of the trust in public institutions, the most important precondition for social progress is the steady accumulation of invisible surplus and development of production forces. Bearing in mind the low levels of capital formation and the high demands for consumption, to prevent private ownership of the means of production, and thereby limiting the extent of that sector's contribution to the creation of wealth and income cannot be defended by involving the principles of socialist direction of society. In the initial stages of creating an independent national economy for countries which do not have a strong and developed capitalism and where the supervision of enterprises therefore is limited by the lack of advanced technical and conscious cadres, the private sector can play a catalytic role so long as the parameters of its operation are clearly spelt out and incentives and reasonable profits are guaranteed by the state. This situation is aggravated by the lack of good traditions of conducting the international affairs of the state, maintaining a proper balance between the state and society and for executing state policy.

The principal constraint is obviously the legacy created by an almost unlimited growth of the public sector in the past. People continue to respect the state to be the sole agency responsible for improvement in their welfare. The result is that they will overload the state with demands and give priority to consumption over production. Thus, in Africa, people consume more and more and produce less and less resulting in Africans in becoming nations of petty traders. Although there is pressure to retrench the state sector, little has been done and many political consequences are potentially hazardous.

In order to change the existing order and to make planning a more broadly based activity representatives of different tendencies, ideologies professions in society should constitute politically independent Planning Commissions, along the lines of an independent judiciary. These commissions would work with government but would above all be charged with ensuring that the people retain control of their economic activities and safeguarding their interests against periodic changes of government and the possibility of retrogressive policies. The setting up of these commissions presupposes a new political thrust by the state, which should promote and safeguard democracy and popular emancipation. A planning Commission, properly constituted, would also play a key role in the development of productive forces, in deciding levels of investment and consumption, location of industries and order of priorities in the different sectors of the economy.

The state cannot serve as the sole entrepreneur in Africa and it has to share the burden of development with other institutions in society. Of special interest are the non-governmental organizations, which have proven effective in mobilizing people and resources on a self-reliance basis. As one type of organization that empowers people, non-governmental organizations, which have proven effective, play a vital role similar to that of pressure groups by establishing lines of communication between state agencies and the people. Being less bureaucratic than government institutions, NGOs normally respond more quickly to appeals and demands from the people and do not have the same internal obstacles as large bureaucracies. NGOs as suggested above, are an important aspect of civil society and one means by which power can be diffused and shared. As service agencies, they often achieve better results than other organizations because they rely on voluntary participation and thus enjoy usually higher levels of motivation.

We are convinced that NGOs will achieve recognition in Africa as they continue to out-perform state agencies in various sectors. By demonstrating their capacity, they create an opportunity for offloading the state in a manner that would be helpful to society. NGOs do not have to be a problem to state. Their presents outside the state sector usually provide government departments with opportunities to link up with local activities that benefit all the government as well as the people.

African governments often prompted by donor agencies have been much inclined to adopt single-track solutions to all problems. Instead of recognizing the value of diversity, they have often pursued uniform policy solutions although they are clumsy and inappropriate. It is my candid opinion that greater flexibility is needed both in policy outlook in organizing delivery of state action. Public officials must be encouraged to seek solutions that are creative and appropriate for each time and location rather than developing a `blue print' and attempt to implement it across the country.

Providing the viability of alternative solutions to state policy is an important means to change the existing outlook. State officials must be made to realize that they do not automatically have the only solutions to society's problems, for instance, in the education and health sectors, new combinations of private and public resources to serve the people should be developed and tried out. Instead of paying for everything, usually the common practice of patronage politics, government should provide matching support and reward communities or institutions that have mobilized local resources and an initial installment.

Although there has been much talk of participation in Africa in the past three decades, little has been done. If anything, popular involvement in public affairs has declined. There is, therefore, the need to ensure that in future, policy processes really start from the people, then go to parliament, and finally back to people again. Policy-making must not be the prerogative of officials only.

Participatory modes of policy making can be evolved by strengthening institutions willing to encourage more democratic practices within state institutions as part of broader democratic practices within society at large. We realize that this is a difficult and far reaching measure that would only become reality in conjunction with the other measures analyzed. It entails reforms in both the economic and political sphere, including breaking the spell of the present neo-colonial order.

It is generally believed that neo-colonialism, more than anything else, holds back Africa's creativity and potential to develop on its own. However, it should also be taken into consideration that Africa's long period of colonialism and colonial domination makes it difficult to crush neo-colonialism as a viper: it will always exist. We shall also practice it against others when Africa becomes strong. The only way to defeat neo-colonialism is to compete with the so-called advanced nations in productivity and we can only do so if we apply to an increasing extent, home-brewed results, science and technology, to agriculture and industry. African Unity can only help if it leads to the attainment of this end.

CHAPTER SIX
THE REVOLUTIONARY DIMENSION

It is true that Africa is still overburdened by the scourge of inherited social ills, be it famine, disease, poverty and any other forms of underdevelopment. This is despite the fact that the continent began the process of decolonization way back in 1957. Although there have been elections all over the continent, but the majority of the African people have been left hungry for true revolutionary change. They want a better continent with an economy fully in their own hands whilst defining their own destiny. They are not hungry for handouts be it from local politicians or from outside donations. Indeed they are hungry for an opportunity to change their own lives. It is only the revolution that can satisfy the aspirations of the people of Africa. This revolution must not be a myth by which African politicians perpetually hoodwink the majority of the people at election times. It must be a revolution which of necessity, transforms the poor into an organized economic force. The force must have as its axis a conscious commitment to genuine wealth creation for the entire continent—a genuine revolutionary desire to ensure broad-based utilization of continental resources for the benefit of everyone. The revolution must not be a front for selfish elites seeking self-aggrandizement in the name of the people. We know that Africa is still smitten by the brutal scourge of corruption among most of its leadership. Until and unless the corrupt lot within the revolution are completely destroyed the cause of the people will continue to be thwarted. The culture of corruption is deeply rooted in the African continent to such an extent that whistle-blowing alone cannot be enough to eliminate the practice. The power to ruthlessly deal with corruption must be within the revolution itself and not only at its top. Thus, crooks must fear the people more than they fear the leader. If we allow people to deal with corrupt elites and other corrupt sectors of the society, then corruption may be reduced to the utmost minimum. Thus, accountability in a revolution is the responsibility of the majority of the people.

It is one thing to come up with high sounding economic and political platitudes; and yet another thing to complete the complex task of fully implementing these policies to their logical and intended end. In fact, in completing the promised tasks African politicians must be reminded that the revolution is not in political power, but that political power is in the revolution. One cannot establish a political base in order to safeguard the revolution; rather one makes a revolution in order to safeguard power. Those in power do not own the revolution. The revolution owns them and can uplift or destroy them. The goals of the revolution must have to be fully and profoundly defined so that the vision of the revolution is so clear that everyone finds cause in pursuing and defending it.

The revolutionary change that is sought in Africa must mark the birth of a new society—a society of progress indigenous producers running the economic affairs of the continent. "We cannot keep talking of a revolution when our politicians are in the notorious habit of addressing rallies comprised of the old colonial servants—resigned to fate, naïve, credulous, slaves of obscurantism, and ferociously submissive to inferiority" (Wafawarova, Herald December 13, 2012). Thus, the revolution must of necessity celebrate the birth of a new society made up of a breed of citizens who are aware of their responsibilities, citizens who are working for the future by pursuing new technologies and facing up to competition in the global market. Only the African can create for Africa an independent economy. The foreign actor cannot by definition create an independent economy for Africa, and history has taught us enough brutal lessons about this. Poverty eradication, not as act of charity or even political benevolence, must take the center stage in African development. It should be born in mind that poverty cannot be ended by giving people money or any other forms of handouts. Most charities today perpetuate poverty more than they try to stop it.
In the African revolution, it must always be remembered that poverty alleviation starts with a transformation of the mindset of the poor and that the implementation of anti-

poverty policies must always involve the active participation of the beneficiaries if the economic handicaps hindering a people's progress are to be removed. Thus, poverty resides more in the mind than it does in its various forms of manifestations; and nothing can be done about eradicating poverty if the mindset of the poor is not transformed. The African people must have a mindset that instructs that poverty cannot be eradicated by the culture of receiving, and that jobs in themselves are never designed to end the poverty of the employed. It is true that jobs can play the crucial role of pacifying the pain of dire poverty by making the employed spend the rest of their lives in the comfort of mild poverty, or if lucky in mild riches, but no job is designed to create wealth for the employed but for the employer. Thus, working classes of Africa must not be so blinded by the need for jobs as to forget that employment creation that does not benefit the continent's people is nothing but a stop gap.

CHAPTER SEVEN
THE WAY I SEE IT

To sum it up, Africa needs capital but she does not need to borrow it. The Soviet Union built up her own capital without any significant borrowing. She made severe sacrifices in order to achieve a better future. Borrowing at every turn cannot solve the African problem. Certainly, judicious borrowing has its place, but indiscriminate soliciting for funds, foreign investment etc. is the beginning of slavery. Colonial regimes built up reserves without borrowing and African countries can also do it.

The other evil contributing to our woes in Africa is our inability to put first things first. The second evil is our almost total lack of appreciation for science education as the bulwark of agriculture and industry.

What are the first things? If we take the example of a tree as an organic unit, the tree is a highly organized industrial unit. Certainly, no human organization can surpass it in efficiency. It works to sustain itself. It does this systematically and orderly. It does not grow flowers first. It does not concern itself with prestige and grandeur until it has secured for itself the life sustaining conditions —

water, carbon dioxide and energy.
From the tree then we learn the next phase of activity that after attaining independence it is not an elaborate foreign service and embassies, not huge armies and novices, not mighty statues and national monuments, not parks and gardens but agriculture, agriculture and industries, industries and industries.

Africa indeed needs industries to convert our minerals into finished products, cocoa into chocolate, tobacco into cigarettes, air into fertilizer, oils into soap, clay into pots and cups. This should be the major activity in Africa. It should utilize the total available energy to create new things out of natural resources to provide the common needs such as food, shelter, clothing and where the raw materials are not available, to exchange some of these finished products for these raw materials and to turn these in turn into more valuable products.

This is the secret of the greatness of the developed nations. They never stand in one place in industry. They are always looking out for opportunity to introduce some useful and imaginative innovations. The more they do this the richer they become and the poorer African, Asian and Latin American nations become. They want transistors, television sets, cameras and even furniture, plates and multitude of other goods, which they cannot make but desire passionately. The irony of it all is that "the made in Britain" etc. goods have their raw materials originating from Africa. When these countries grow richer we go to the United Nations to complain that we are becoming poorer and poorer. These nations see it, but there is nothing they can do about it. They just cannot toil for Africa. And just as the rich man throws a cent to the beggar at the street corner, so do our former colonial masters give to us some pittance or loans with unbreakable strings.

Africa would fail were it not for its virtually inexhaustible resources. The sun alone is a source of incalculable wealth. Then when we are well-fed, adequately clothed and comfortably housed we can turn to litany and cultural activities; we can turn to literature and philosophy, to drumming and dancing, to radio and television, we can turn to large armies and navies, to the air force and new missiles.

We can turn to statues and monuments to white elephants and red lions as America, indeed, has done because at that time we can afford.

The order of priorities then is first agriculture and fishing, secondly mining and industry and lastly literary and cultural activities. In this way Africa would have put first things first and succeeded in laying a solid foundation for sustained growth.

If Africa would conceive this and above all our leaders

grasp this phenomenon, Africa's poverty, disease and unending internal strife would vanish. A new era would have been ushered in and the black man would have taken his rightful place in the community of nations. Indeed, what is it that keeps our leaders in a state of humiliating reliance on Western aid? Why do the educated classes of Africa spend so much time demanding the crumbs of materialistic prestige to be snatched from Europe and America, and so little developing local resources such as agriculture? The answer as suggested by Frantz Fanon is that the governing class of our countries has so far so long left the responsibility of its decisions to others that it is now deprived of the capacity to take any constructive initiative since it implies a minimum of risk. The failure is one of imagination. The people lost the capacity to improvise since they no longer possess the necessary confidence in the creative potential of their own culture. We must indeed rise to a pitch of equality with the rest of the world.